MCR

What's the Plan?

Designing Your Experiment

Natalie Hyde

Science education consultant: Suzy Gazlay

Crabtree Publishing Company

www.crabtreebooks.com

Crabtree Publishing Company

www.crabtreebooks.com

Author: Natalie Hyde
Series editor: Vashti Gwynn
Editorial director: Paul Humphrey
Editor: Adrianna Morganelli
Proofreader: Reagan Miller
Production coordinator: Katherine Berti
Prepress technician: Katherine Berti
Project manager: Kathy Middleton
Illustration: Stefan Chabluk and Stuart Harrison
Photography: Chris Fairclough
Cover design: Katherine Berti
Design: sprout.uk.com
Photo research: Vashti Gwynn

Produced for Crabtree Publishing Company by Discovery Books.

Thanks to models Ottilie and Sorcha Austin-Baker, Dan Brice-Bateman, Matthew Morris, and Amrit and Tara Shoker.

Photographs:
Alamy: Emmanuel Lattes: p. 23
California Institute of Technology (Courtesy of
the Archives): p. 19 (right)
Corbis: Jim Craigmyle: p. 20 (bottom)
Discovery Photo Library: Chris Fairclough: p. 6 (right),
17 (bottom), 22, 27 (top)
Istockphoto: Red Helga: p. 13 (left); ElementalImaging:
p. 16 (left); Mr Loz: p. 18; Julof90: p. 25 (left)
NASA: p. 9, 11, 27 (bottom)
Samara Parent: back cover, p. 1 (top)
Science Photo Library: p. 13 (right)
Shutterstock: cover, p. 1 (center left and center right),
3, 8 (top), 10 (bottom left), 15 (bottom left), 21 (right),
25 (top right), 26 (top right), 28 (bottom right);
Rich Carey: p. 4 (bottom left); Weldon Schloneger:
p. 7 (bottom); Jan Schuler: p. 8 (bottom); Damien
Herde: p. 10 (right); Dole: p. 17 (top); Robert
Redelowski: p. 20 (top); Orhan Çam: p. 26 (bottom);
Matt Antonino: p. 28 (left)

Library and Archives Canada Cataloguing in Publication

Hyde, Natalie, 1963-
    What's the plan? Designing your experiment / Natalie Hyde.

(Step into science)
Includes index.
ISBN 978-0-7787-5154-0 (bound).--ISBN 978-0-7787-5169-4 (pbk.)

        1. Science--Methodology--Juvenile literature. 2. Science--
Experiments--Juvenile literature. I. Title. II. Series: Step into
science (St. Catharines, Ont.)

Q175.2.H93 2010   j507.8   C2009-906460-X

Library of Congress Cataloging-in-Publication Data

Challen, Paul C. (Paul Clarence), 1967-
  What's going to happen? Making your hypothesis / Paul Challen.
    p. cm. -- (Step into science)
  Includes index.
  ISBN 978-0-7787-5157-1 (reinforced lib. bdg. : alk. paper)
  -- ISBN 978-0-7787-5172-4 (pbk. : alk. paper)
  1. Science--Methodology--Juvenile literature. 2. Hypothesis--Juvenile
literature. I. Title. II. Series.

  Q175.2.C4274 2010
  507.8--dc22

                                                    2009044174

Crabtree Publishing Company

Printed in the U.S.A./122009/CG20091120

www.crabtreebooks.com   1-800-387-7650

Published in Canada
Crabtree Publishing
616 Welland Ave.
St. Catharines, Ontario
L2M 5V6

Published in the United States
Crabtree Publishing
PMB 59051
350 Fifth Avenue, 59th Floor
New York, New York 10118

Published in the United Kingdom
Crabtree Publishing
Maritime House
Basin Road North, Hove
BN41 1WR

Published in Australia
Crabtree Publishing
386 Mt. Alexander Rd.
Ascot Vale (Melbourne)
VIC 3032

CONTENTS

THE SCIENTIFIC METHOD

Have you ever been in an elevator? The **scientific method** is like an elevator—you enter at the first floor and take the elevator up. The elevator passes one floor at a time, and you get closer and closer to your final stop. Sometimes, however, the journey takes you back down before you continue on to reach your destination.

In the same way, following each step in the scientific method is important for making scientific discoveries. Sometimes, though, scientists have to stop, go back, and think again before they continue.

This book will look at how to plan an experiment. There are many things you need to think about. How will you set up your experiment? How long will it take? What tools do you need? These are some of the questions you will need to answer. Careful planning will ensure your experiment is a success!

◄ Marine biologists study underwater plants and animals. This marine biologist is investigating a lionfish.

Beginning Your Scientific Investigation

Be curious! Questions can come from anywhere, anytime. Questions help scientists make **observations** and do **research**. Science is all about problem-solving!

Making Your Hypothesis

So, what is next? You have a question, and you have done some research. You think you know what will happen when you perform your experiment. The term *hypothesis* means educated guess. So, make a guess and get started!

Designing Your Experiment

How are you going to test your hypothesis? Designing a safe, accurate experiment will give **results** that answer your question.

Collecting and Recording Your Data

During an experiment, scientists make careful observations and record exactly what happens.

Displaying and Understanding Results

Now your **data** can be organized into **graphs, charts,** and diagrams. These help you read the information, think about it, and figure out what it means.

Making Conclusions and Answering the Question

So, what did you learn during your experiment? Did your data prove your hypothesis? Scientists share their results so other scientists can try out the experiment, or use the results to try another experiment.

WHAT KIND OF EXPERIMENT?

There are different kinds of experiments. One type looks at what something does when it is treated in different ways. For instance, you might wonder what would happen if you put cut white daisies in different liquids. You would put some daisies in water, some in water with blue food coloring, some in lemonade, and some in milk. Then you would see what happened.

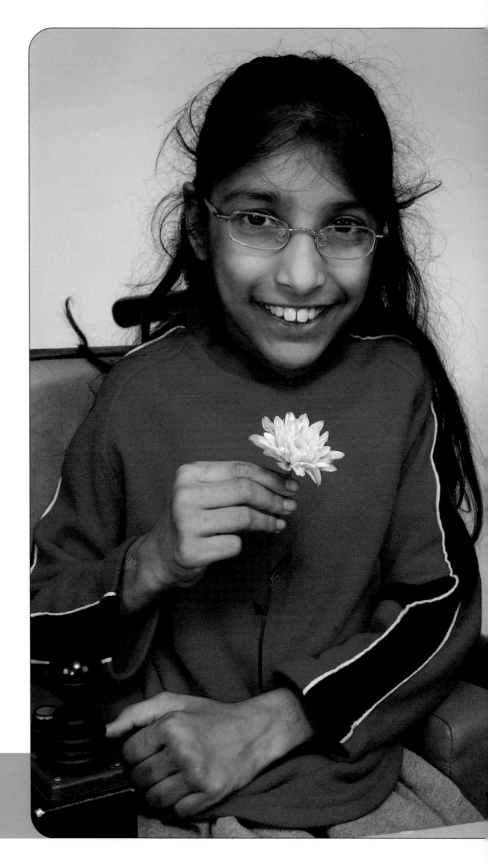

▶ An experiment can help prove what made these flower petals turn blue.

Another type of experiment looks at what different things do when treated the same way. You might have discovered that putting white daisies in water with blue food coloring turns their petals blue. Now you might be wondering whether that would happen with all types of flowers. You would put several different cut flowers in water with blue food coloring to see what happened.

Bruneau made a very cool discovery!

Ice Race!

Dr. Stephen Bruneau is an iceberg expert. He lives in Newfoundland, Canada. He wondered if iceberg ice melted faster than ice made from tap water. He designed an experiment to find out. He collected a small piece of an iceberg. He made an ice block using tap water that was the same size and shape as his iceberg sample. He let both pieces melt under the same **conditions**. He noted that the iceberg ice melted a little bit faster than the tap water ice.

VARIABLES

A **variable** is something that can change. There are two kinds of variables in experiments. One is changed by the scientist. This is called the **independent variable**. In the daisy experiment described on page six, the independent variable is the type of liquid. The scientist uses different liquids to see what will happen. In the experiment on page seven, the independent variable is the types of plants that the scientist uses in the experiment.

▼ Many different variables affect flowers that grow naturally. Weather, soil, and insects can change how large or fast they grow.

In every experiment the independent variable might make something else change. The thing it changes is also a variable. It is called the **dependent variable**. In the experiment on page six, the scientist is observing the color of the petals. The independent variable (the type of liquid) changes the dependent variable (the color of the petals).

A good experiment only looks at one dependent variable at a time. This way you can be more certain of the result.

Go to Bed!

How would you like to stay in bed for a year? That's what 11 men in Russia did. It was an experiment conducted by a scientist named Boris Morukov. He wanted to see what happens to the human body in space where there isn't any gravity. He thought lying down for a long time would have a similar effect, so that's what the men did. They ate, washed, and watched TV in bed. Morukov studied the changes in the men's muscles. This was one of the dependent variables.

▲ Dr. Mae Jemison is a NASA astronaut. Like Boris Murokov, she did experiments to understand how astronauts' bodies change during space flight. Here, she is working aboard Spacelab *Japan*.

MANY OR FEW?

Every experiment uses **samples**. Samples are the things you are experimenting on. In the experiments on pages six and seven, the plants are the samples.

How many samples should you use? This is an important decision in planning your experiment. Imagine you are doing the daisy experiment on page six. You might think you should have just one daisy in each type of liquid. In fact, you should have several daisies in each type of liquid. Then you can compare them all to see if they all change in the same way.

▶ These pots of barley sprouts are being tested for disease. Scientists use hundreds of samples to check their results.

Space Seeds

Since 2007, schools in the United States have been able to get some very special basil seeds from **NASA**. These seeds were stored outside the International Space Station (below) for a year. Students will plant the space seeds and compare them to seeds stored on Earth. This experiment can help scientists plan space missions. On some trips astronauts will need to grow their own food. Scientists wonder how well seeds grow when they have been carried in space. The results from this experiment will give them important information.

Imagine the petals on all the daisies in the water with blue food coloring turned blue, and none in the other liquids did. Then you could be certain that it was the type of liquid causing the change. This means you could be sure that it was your independent variable causing your dependent variable to change.

CONTROLS

A **control** is a sample with no independent variable. It is a way to make sure your results are not an accident. There should be a control sample in each experiment. The independent variable in the control should not change.

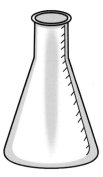

◄ The control sample is one of the most important parts of your experiment. Without it you cannot prove your results. This boy is putting a daisy into clear water as his control sample.

Lind's sour experiment had sweet results!

James Lind

In the 1700s, James Lind (above) was a ship's doctor. The crew was very sick. They had a disease called **scurvy**. This disease gave them spots on their legs and made their teeth fall out. He gave the sick sailors different treatments. He tried **cider**, seawater, vinegar, and lemons. Some sailors received no treatment. These sailors were his control samples. He noticed that only the sailors having lemons were getting better. His experiment showed that lemons cured scurvy.

In the daisy experiment on page six, one flower should be put in clear water. This is your control sample. The petals on this flower should stay white. This will show that daisy petals don't normally turn blue. That means it was the color of the liquid that caused the petals to change color.

LET'S EXPERIMENT!

Magnetic Paper Clips

Problem

Some metals are attracted to magnets. In this experiment we can ask, how many paper clips does one magnet hold? Will two magnets hold twice as many paper clips?

1 Open up one paper clip to form a hook.

2 Hold up one magnet and stick the paper clip "hook" to it. Add paper clips one at a time to the hook. Make a tally to record the number of paper clips added to the hook.

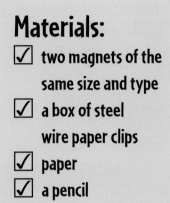

3 Keep adding paper clips until your hook falls. Don't count the paper clip that makes the hook fall. Add up your tallies.

4 Now stick a second magnet behind the first. Keep the paper clip hook on the outside of the magnet. Don't sandwich it in between the two magnets.

5 How many paper clips do you think your two magnets will hold? Start adding your paper clips to find out! Remember to keep a tally.

Do You have a Plan?

There are some things to think about when planning this experiment. You have to make sure all the paper clips are the same size. What about the size of the magnets? Does it matter how big or small they are? Does it matter whether the magnets are the same size?

TOOLS OF THE TRADE

Part of your plan should be what **equipment** you will need. For instance, you need to think about what you're going to put your samples in and what you might need for your independent variable. You must also plan how you're going to measure your results.

If you are measuring how high or wide something is, you will need a tape measure or ruler.

For liquids, you will need measuring cups or spoons. A scale is needed to weigh things. If you are timing anything you will need a stopwatch or a clock with a second hand. You can use a camera to take pictures or a notepad to draw diagrams.

It is important to make sure your equipment is clean. Dust, dirt, or rust could change the results of your experiment. If your experiment is messy, you should protect the area with newspaper, cloth, or plastic.

▼ Beakers and flasks are glasses used for mixing, measuring, and heating liquids.

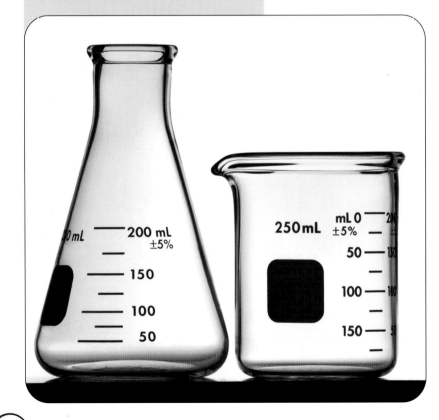

Use tools like these for good measure!

◀ Measurements can be made in metric units (grams, centimeters, and liters) or imperial units (pounds, inches, and ounces).

It is good to think about protecting your clothes from damage, too. You need to think about protecting yourself as well. Will you need gloves or goggles?

Follow the Rules

Most laboratories have safety rules. These rules are made to protect scientists. Here are some rules you should follow when you're experimenting:

- Always check with a parent or teacher before starting an experiment;

- Have an adult help with sharp tools;

- If you don't know what something is, never touch, taste, or smell it;

- Never fool around;

- Report all spills or accidents to a parent or teacher;

- Make sure you have all the safety equipment you need.

▼ A stopwatch is a good tool for measuring things that happen quickly.

WHERE ARE YOU?

You will need a special place to do your experiment. It should be near the equipment you will be using. Lights or heaters will need electricity. A spot near a radiator will be warm.

The basement might be good for darkness. Make sure all your samples are kept under the same condition, apart from the independent variable you want to change.

▼ A quiet corner in a classroom can be a good spot for an experiment.

The Fly Room

Thomas Hunt Morgan found the perfect spot for his experiment: in a room at Columbia University. He was studying how eye color was passed from parent to offspring. He used fruit flies. They are the little insects that fly around old or rotting fruit. Morgan needed thousands and thousands of samples. He bred the fruit flies in milk bottles to study how eye color was passed on. Bunches of rotting bananas hung from the ceiling, to be used as food for the fruit flies. Everyone at the university called it "The Fly Room."

The best spot is where the experiment won't be disturbed. It may have to be there for quite a while. You don't want anyone to accidentally knock things over or step on them. You also don't want to damage the area. You should always get permission before you set up your experiment.

Morgan carefully planned his experiment—he didn't "wing" it!

▶ Thomas Hunt Morgan won the Nobel Prize for his experiments on fruit flies.

IT'S ABOUT TIME

It is important to plan for enough time to do your experiment. Rushing through an experiment can cause accidents. Some experiments take a long time. For instance, growing, melting, and **rusting** may happen very slowly.

▶ An experiment with rusting might take weeks or months.

▼ The position of stars in the sky changes as Earth moves around the Sun. It would take an entire year to watch the stars circle back to where they started.

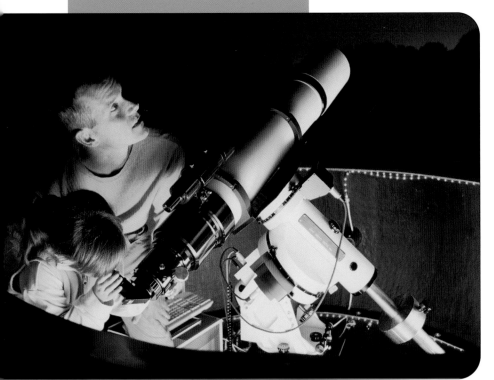

How will you know when your experiment is finished? Some experiments are over when something stops happening. If you are melting ice, the experiment is done when the ice is gone.

Yawn!

The longest running experiment in the world is still going. It is the pitch drop experiment. Pitch is the same as blacktop: the sticky, black material used to pave driveways. An Australian scientist named Professor Thomas Parnell began the experiment in 1927. He wanted to see how long it would take for a jar of pitch to drip out of the jar. Pitch is very thick and gooey and moves very slowly. One drop falls about every eight years. Scientists guess it will take at least another hundred years for the jar to empty.

The Pitch Drop Experiment

1927	Experiment set up
1930	Pitch started to flow
1938 Dec	1st drop fell
1947 Feb	2nd drop fell
1954 Apr	3rd drop fell
1962 May	4th drop fell
1970 Aug	5th drop fell
1979 Apr	6th drop fell
1988 Jul	7th drop fell
2000 Nov	8th drop fell
2009 Mar	9th drop fell

Others could go on for a long time. Plants will keep growing, maybe for years. For that type of experiment you should decide how long to continue. You do not want to stop your experiment too soon. This might give you a false result.

WHAT DO YOU SEE?

Observations are what you notice ishappening. To make an observation you can think about what you can see or hear. Sometimes, you can use touch, taste, or smell as well. Be careful not to touch, taste, or smell something unknown, though. However you make your observations, you need to make them accurately.

One way to make accurate observations is to make observations at the same time each day. This will help you to remember. Forgetting to observe your experiment could mean that you miss something important. It will also show you how slowly or quickly something is changing.

Make insightful observations!

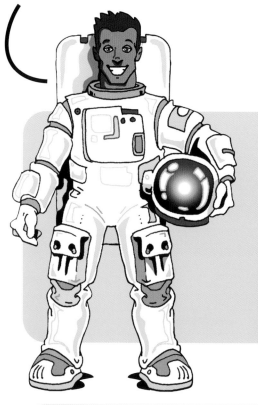

▶ A magnifying glass can help you observe changes that are very small.

Another way to be accurate is to make observations under the same conditions. You might measure a plant's growth one hour after watering. Or, you might count the number of ducklings living in your local lake every spring. Whatever way you choose, you should do the same thing all the way through the experiment.

Fast Fact
The giant timber **bamboo** is the fastest growing plant on Earth. It can grow nearly four feet (over a meter) a day! If you were studying how fast this bamboo grew you would take measurements more often. You could take them every hour instead of every day.

▼ A bamboo plant in Japan produced a cane that grew 47 inches (120 cm) in 24 hours! You could measure this plant's growth every hour.

LET'S EXPERIMENT!

Chalk Chomp

Materials:
- ☑ three jars
- ☑ lemon juice
- ☑ vinegar
- ☑ water
- ☑ three long pieces of white chalk
- ☑ a ruler

Problem
Acids are chemicals that destroy certain things. In this experiment we will determine which liquid—vinegar, water, or lemon juice—is a stronger acid. What do you think?

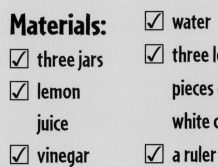

1 Put one piece of chalk in each jar.

2 Pour lemon juice in one jar, vinegar in another, and plain water in another. Pour in enough liquid to cover the chalk. Make sure you use the same amount of liquid in each jar.

3 Check the jars every hour for a day or two. Write down your observations. You can also draw what you see, or measure each piece of chalk with a ruler.

◄ Because of pollution, there is acid in rainfall. This statue has been damaged by acid rain.

Watch It!

It is important to make your observations every hour. If you only check once a day, all three pieces of chalk may be gone and you will not know which one dissolved the fastest. Make sure you write down all the details that you can. This will help you compare the different samples at the end of the experiment.

NOW WHAT?

You've found the perfect time and the perfect place. You have all your equipment and your samples ready. You've drawn your tables and are ready to start observing. It's time to begin your experiment!

▼ Observing and recording what happens in an experiment is the exciting part for scientists.

▲ There are still many discoveries waiting to be made.

In the next step of the scientific method, a scientist observes his or her experiment very closely and records data. Good planning will mean a great experiment with no mistakes. Have a look through your **journal** (see pages 28-29) to make sure you've followed every step of your plan. Now you'll see science in action!

Hubble Telescope

The Hubble Telescope circles Earth every 97 minutes. It orbits in space above the atmosphere, where it can take clear photos of stars and galaxies like these ones. It is a floating data collector.

KEEPING A JOURNAL

Imagine if your friend is telling you how to get to his house. The directions he's giving are very complicated. You're sure you won't be able to remember them.

What would you do? You'd write it all down, of course! For scientists, a journal is like directions for how to get to their conclusion.

A journal can be anything from a scrapbook, to a binder with lined paper, from a computer file, to a notepad! The important thing about a journal is that it is where scientists record everything about their experiment, from beginning to end.

◀ Everything from notes and thoughts, to drawings and pictures can be included in your journal.

Your journal is a great place to plan your experiment. Putting your plan on paper will help you remember all the steps. You can write down where and when you are going to do your experiment. You can also make a note of all the equipment you are going to use. If you have a problem, re-reading your plan will help you decide where to change things.

My Science Journal:
Chalks and Acids Continued

Research
My Mom told me that some common liquids are acid. She said some juices and vinegars might react with the chalk.

* Day 2. March 15, 20

Hypothesis
The lemon juice will dissolve the chalk fastest, followed by the vinegar. Tap water will dissolve the chalk slowest.

* Day 3. March 16, 20

Procedure
I will put a stick of chalk in three jars. Then I will add vinegar to the first one, lemon juice to the second, and tap water to the third. I will be careful to use the same amount of liquid in each jar.

Vinegar   Lemon   Water

I will put the jars somewhere they won't be disturbed, and I will check them every hour. Each time I will measure each piece of chalk, and write down all my observations in my journal.

▲ Here is an example of a well-planned experiment. It is neatly recorded in the scientist's journal.

Here are some Tips for Keeping Your Journal:

- Make sure you write the date every time you use your journal;

- Make sure you write clearly, so that you'll be able to read your notes later on;

- If you are going to record your results in a table, draw it before you start your experiment;

- If your experiment set-up is complicated, you can draw a diagram of your experiment. This is a neat drawing of exactly what goes where. Make sure you use labels!

You must take the time to make a plan, so your experiment doesn't end up in the garbage can!

TIMELINE

Below is a list of scientific discoveries and inventions that needed careful planning.

Year	Discovery or invention	What was the plan?
900s	Controlling the Nile floods	Alhazen doesn't plan very well when he boasts he can stop the Nile River from flooding. He spends the rest of his life pretending to be mad, in case he is in trouble!
1200s	How rainbows are created	Al-Farisi's experiment needs careful planning, because he has to build a giant raindrop for it. Then he can make his own rainbows.
1666	That flies lay eggs which become maggots	Francesco Redi is very careful to only change one variable when he does his experiments. He lets flies land on some samples of rotting meat and not others.
1866	How traits are passed from parent to young	Gregor Mendel studies around 29,000 pea plants over seven years. Now that's a lot of samples!
1964	How dolphins communicate	Wayne Batteau needs a very special place to keep his samples. They are two dolphins called Maui and Puka!
1999	Studying Oklahoma tornadoes	The VORTEX-99 team has mobile laboratories. They chase tornadoes in cars filled with special equipment!
2003	Monitoring Mount Cayley volcano	Catherine Hickson has to be especially careful with safety planning when she studies a large Canadian volcano.

GLOSSARY

bamboo A plant that has a hard, woody stem

chart A way of showing numbers in rows and columns. Also called a table

cider An alcoholic beverage made from pressing apples

conditions The state something is in

control A sample without any independent variable

data Scientific information

dependent variable The changing thing about your samples

equipment All the physical things you need to do your experiment

graph A diagram that can illustrate the results of an experiment. A graph has one measurement along the bottom, and another up the side

hypothesis An educated guess about what an experiment will prove

independent variable The thing that you change so that you can see the effect on your samples

journal A record of every step of an experiment

NASA National Aeronautics and Space Administration: the American space agency

observation Noticing things happening by using the five senses

research Finding out facts about something

results The information that comes from an experiment

rust Something that happens to metal when it is in contact with air and water for a long time

sample A piece of the thing you're testing

scientific method The way to do an experiment properly

scurvy An illness caused by lack of Vitamin C

variable Something that changes in an experiment

FURTHER INFORMATION

Books
Pop Bottle Science, Lynn Brunelle, Workman Publishing Company, September 2004

Science Through the Ages, Janice VanCleave, Wiley, July 2002

Web sites
www.nasa.gov/audience/foreducators/plantgrowth/home/index.html
NASA Seeds in Space Program

www.sciencebob.com/index.php

INDEX